I0530474

MATRESCENCE

The transition from woman to mother
Raw, honest, unfiltered moments of the first five years

Matrescence © 2025 Morgan Davis

All rights reserved.

No part of this publication may be reproduced, distributed, or transmitted in any form or by any means, including photocopying, recording, or other electronic or mechanical methods, without the prior written permission of the publisher, except in the case of brief quotations used in reviews or scholarly works.

Published by Soft Echo Press

ISBN: 979-8-9992020-0-0

First edition

Illustrations by Anna Shepherd

Cover design by Anna Shepherd

This is a work of poetry. Any references to real people, living or dead, are purely coincidental.

Printed by independent print services.

For Mrs. Eichner —
thank you for believing in me since first grade.

For Kolin —
my anchor, my best friend, my soulmate.

And for Grace —
my muse, my why, my everything.

Preface

Matrescence is the word we never learned but always needed.

It describes the transformation a woman undergoes as she
becomes a mother — physically, emotionally, mentally, and
spiritually. Like adolescence, it is profound, disorienting, and
often invisible to those around us.

This collection traces my own matrescence through the first five
years of motherhood.

From the moment I felt the call to become a mother, through the
fog of postpartum, to the bittersweet clarity of watching my
daughter turn five — these poems are a record of my becoming.

These poems are honest. At times, they are raw. They are not
always polished, just as motherhood is not. You'll find joy here,
yes — but also grief, rage, wonder, and awe.

This is a love letter to my daughter.
A reclamation of my voice.
And a tribute to every mother who has felt herself unravel and
rebuild, over and over again.

If you find yourself within these pages — know you are not
alone.

We were never meant to do this alone.

The Calling

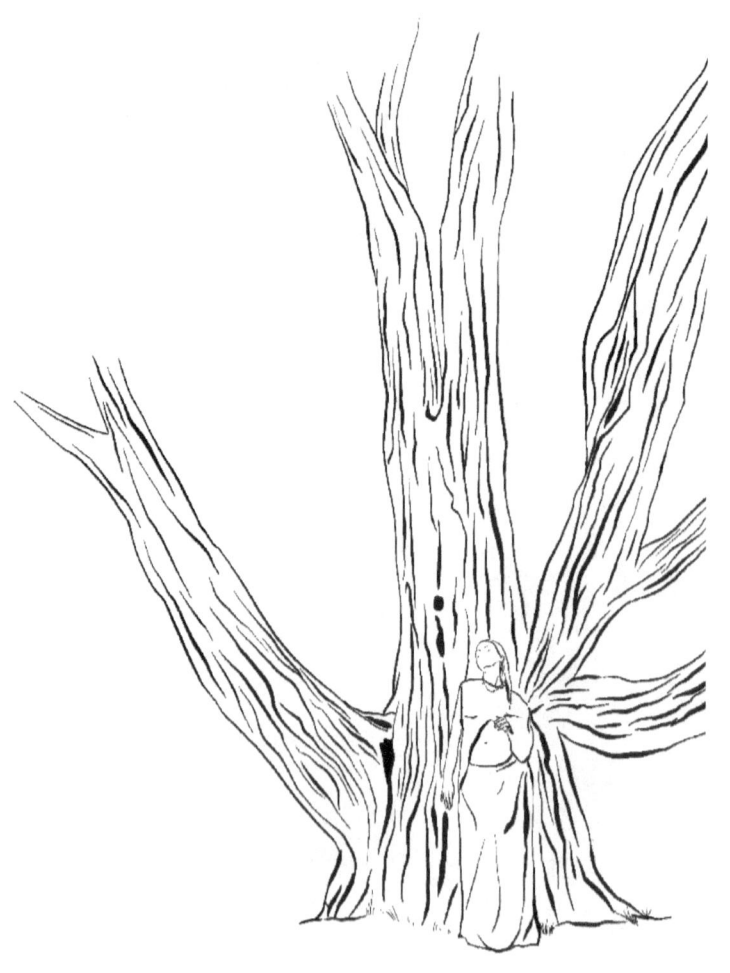

The Decision

I am ready,
for something greater,
something bigger than myself.

Like a download from the divine
an invitation from a higher power,
saying it's time.

Motherhood knocking on my doorstep,
a calling I must answer,
a primal urge I cannot explain.

Yes, I say,

I am ready,
for something greater,
something bigger than myself.

Among the Cheers

Another pregnancy announcement.
Joy spreads like wildfire,
cheers fill the room.

My heart sinks,
as I plaster on a smile
and embrace you in a hug.

"Congratulations," I say,
tears escaping down my cheeks.

You think it's from happiness,
but I know it's from sorrow.

Shame fills my chest.
I want to be happy for you—
I do.

But the weight of disappointment
is slowly suffocating me.

The Tests

Another month,
another negative.

It's fine,
I tell myself.

There's no rush,
I tell myself.

But I know—
I know the call of Motherhood
is no longer knocking.

She's pounding,
demanding to be let in.

The Tests (Continued)

This desire,
no longer a whisper,
but a primal scream.

I'm trying,
I scream back.

I'm trying,
I whisper,

as I gently toss
another failed test
into the trash.

The Mask

After five minutes of limbo,
I throw away another test—
another negative,
like the rest.

Heart deflated,
mind numb,
I slip on my shoes
and head out the door.

Thoughts drowning
in a sea of defeat,
I whisper to myself,
"Let's do this."

The Mask (Continued)

At work,
I force a smile.

"How are you?"
they always ask—

the innocent small talk
I try to avoid.

"Another beautiful day,"
I say with delight,
not allowing the mask
to slip from its place.

Only eight more hours,
I think,
as I pass a mirror
and fail to recognize
the woman looking back.

Suddenly

And suddenly,
without warning,
the world tilts.

Everything you thought you knew
shifts in an instant.

You can spend months preparing—

planning,
trying,
praying—

only to realize
no one is ever truly ready
when the call is finally answered.

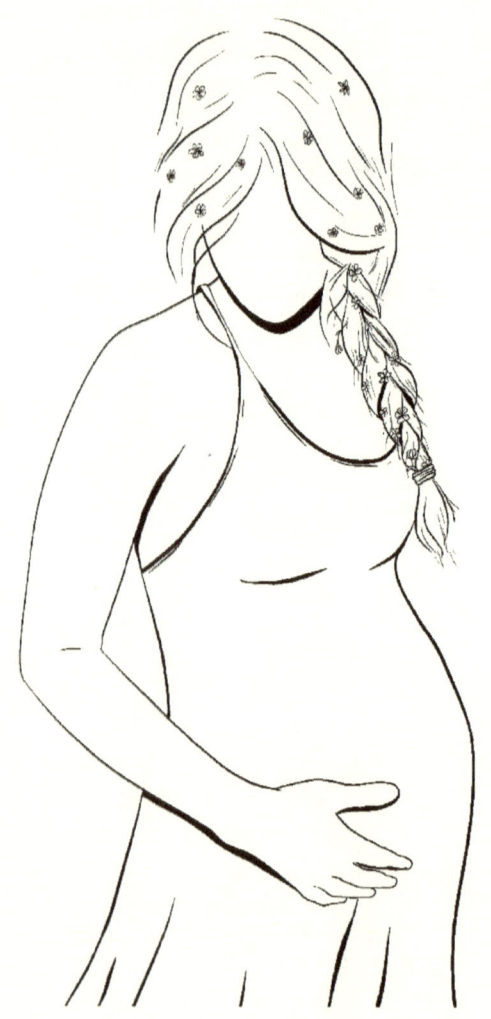

Becoming

The Positive

My body bubbles with elation,
I smile,
I squeal.

I want to burst out my door,
scream down the streets,
thank the heavens.

Oh my God,
I'm pregnant.

Wait, what?

Do I want this?
Holy shit—
a human.

What did we just do?
Fuck.
A life altering decision
you cannot take back.

The Positive (Continued)

Nerves threaten to creep in,
but I push them back.
Fear of the unknown
no longer dictating my life.

A sly smile crawls across my face.
Motherhood is here.
The door wide open.
And I can finally let her in.

Silenced by Society

I want to shout it from the rooftops,
but instead, I say nothing.
Just in case.

Just in case it slips away,
and I am left to grieve alone.

Because apparently,
no one wants to hear
about the heartache,
the guilt.

Apparently,
society would rather I stay quiet—
as I grieve a soul I created,
wondering if it was my fault.

Apparently,
society would rather be blind,
than inconvenienced.

So I tell no one,
as I grow another soul,
suppressing my joy
for the comfort of others.

New Soul

In the silence,
a new soul stirs.

She demands to be known,
refuses to be hidden—
and I agree.

If you wish to share in my joy,
you must also stand beside me in my fear.

Society and I
never got along anyway.

The Connection

There is no bump yet,
but I hold my belly anyway,
silently saying hello.

You tell me what I should eat,
and what I definitely cannot,
and I giggle at the weird suggestions.

How is it that you're the size of a peanut,
yet already my best friend?
This connection, I do not understand.

Your dad walks by,
and kisses my cheek,
placing his hand over mine.

I smile because he feels it too,
this subtle shift in the air,
the sense of responsibility budding.

The Connection (Continued)

How are you barely visible,
yet already altering our identities?
A divine thread connects us three
in a way I didn't know was possible.

Your dad and I lock eyes,
the thread glowing brighter.
If this isn't magic,
I don't know what is.

Brick by Brick

The divine thread between us tightens—
solidifying.

Years spent laying,
brick by brick,
a home within each other—
preparing us for this.

Unknowingly,
preparing it for her.

And now, together,
we rise—
as one.

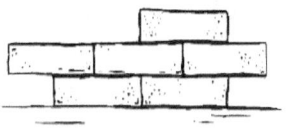

A Rollercoaster

Paper crinkles underneath me
as I take a deep breath
and try to stay calm.

I notice the air is too cold,
the room too sterile,
and the nurse too quiet.

I squeeze your hand tighter,
your thumb rubs along mine.
The walls feel like they're closing in.

"There she is,"
the nurse says,
as a steady heartbeat fills the room.

A Rollercoaster (Continued)

Tears escape my eyes,
as I see you wipe away yours,
and release a sigh.

Elation instantly fills the room,
as if I was not about to suffocate
just moments ago.

A wave of assurance flows through me,
hope blooming in my chest,
which will keep me steady
until our next appointment.

Song of Life

A sound that changes everything.
The song of life.

A sound that makes me a mother,
not just a wife.

A sound that gives us hope,
a song of the soul.

A song for your father and I,
that makes us feel whole.

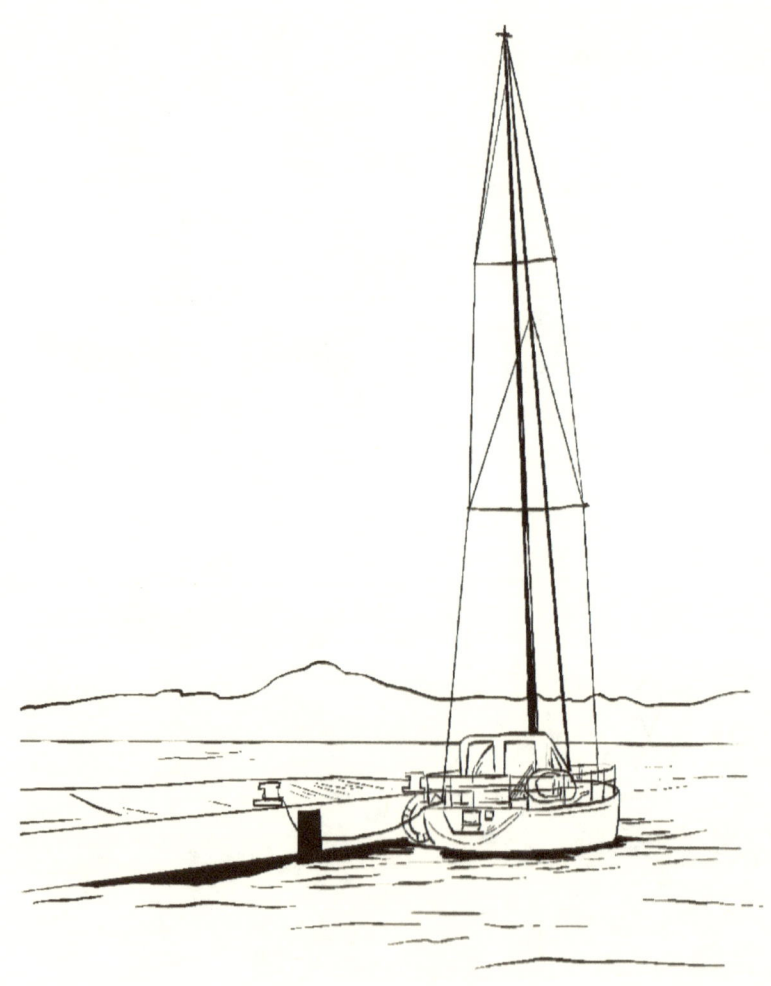

My Anchor

We hear her heartbeat,
I see you quickly wipe a tear,
as our eyes slowly meet.

What a weight you must carry,
suppressing your feelings
to keep mine light and airy.

I'm transforming,
but so are you—
my anchor deserves support too.

So I squeeze your hand tighter,
and bring it to my lips.

Let me be your harbor
for when your strength slips.

Foundation

I hold you,
and you hold me.

A tender love
she'll always see.

Oh, how lucky
our daughter will be.

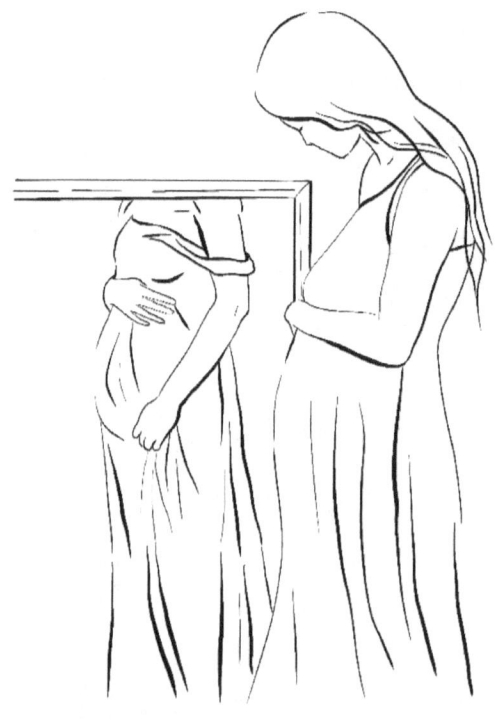

The Bump

The wood floors creak
as I step into your room once again,
my arm resting on the shelf of my belly.

My eyes slowly scan the room—
clean, neat, and organized.
A sense of perfection
that only nesting can bring.

As I walk past your mirror,
I see my reflection and smile.
An ancient energy
attributing to this glow.

This belly feels sacred,
as if the power of the heavens
flows through my veins.

The Bump (Continued)

I allow myself to enjoy this,
these moments of Before,
where confidence is constant
and stress is low.

Blissfully ignorant
of how much life
is about to change.

Rude Awakening

Nothing has changed,
except my silhouette.

I spend my days
doing what I want,
when I want.

Eating up
the congratulations
and compliments
along the way.

Waited on
hand and foot
by father-to-be.

Completely naïve
to how temporary
this all is.

A rude awakening
rises on the horizon,

but still, I skip along
the blissful path of before.

The Next Chapter

I have loved being your home,
protecting you from within.

Feeling you move,
having you close,
keeping you to myself.

And maybe—
maybe I am a little scared
of what's to come.

I know I'll love
this next chapter,
and yet—
I'm still quite sad

that this one
is coming to a close.

Birth

The Contractions

And all of a sudden, we're here—
the beginning of the end,
a new chapter about to unfold.

Contractions intensify,
I take a look at our home
one last time.

Melancholic nostalgia
hits like a tidal wave.
Tears prickle my eyes.

This version of us
is coming to a close.
An unknown path lies ahead.

As we race to the hospital,
I squeeze your hand,
excitement and fear filling the air.

Shock

One second we're checking in—
the next, you're on my chest.

I should be crying tears of joy,
instead of feeling so compressed.

My brain has not yet processed
what has just transpired.

I look into your eyes,
and yet, all I feel is tired.

I want to feel elated
as they teach me how to feed.

But all I feel is numb,
what is wrong with me?

Observer

They take you across the room.
to see how much you weigh.

Even though it will be quick,
I ache for you to stay.

You open your big eyes
and take a look around.

Absorbing your surroundings,
not making a sound.

Slow, steady blinks,
perfectly content.

And even in that moment,
I knew what that meant.

You will be my little observer,
reflective.
aware.

I watch you in awe,
as you peacefully stare.

Disbelief

Sitting here in disbelief,
going through the motions.

Learning how to nurse,
a flood of mixed emotions.

Staring at this human
I'm now responsible for,

confidence long gone—
I've never felt this young before.

I'm supposed to take this home
and just know what to do?

I feel like a child myself—
what the hell did we just do?

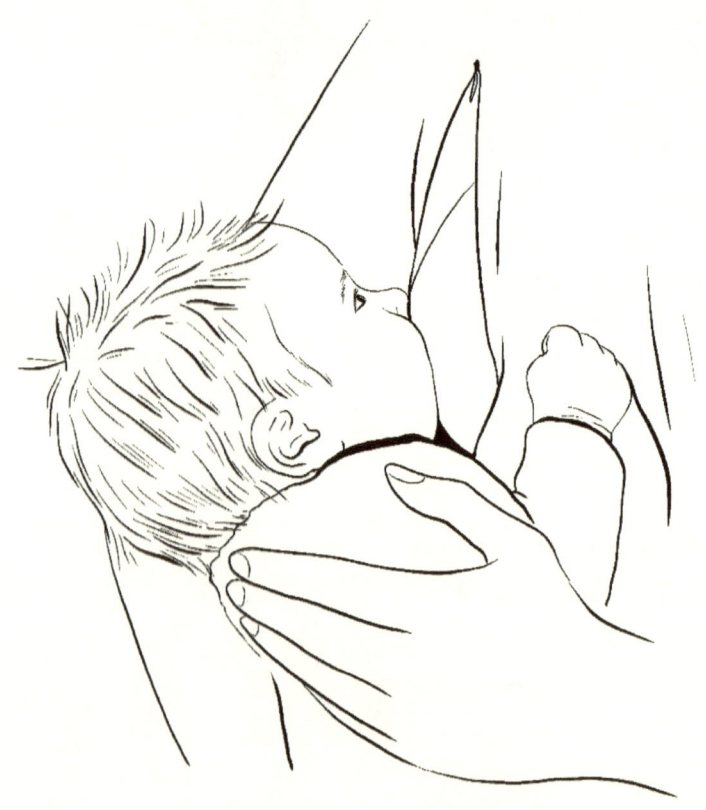

Delirious

A nurse comes in
every few hours
to make sure she feeds.

I've been awake
for two days straight—
what about my needs?

First Bath

I slowly lower myself into the warm water,
hissing—reminded of all that's still healing.

I take in the view of the hospital bathroom,
trying to ignore its cold, sterile presence.

Through a crack in the door,
my eyes find you and your dad.

He holds you gently,
gazing into your eyes,
as tears pour from his.

His shoulders shake,
as relief finally hits him.

First Bath (Continued)

His two most prized possessions—
Healthy.
Alive.

I look away,
as understanding hits me:

how long he's been hiding
his fear for this day—
of losing you,
of losing me.

My throat constricts,
as I hold back tears.
And for a long, quiet moment,
I thank the powers above
for getting us here.

Take Us Home

The moment they say we can leave,
we're packing up our bags—

how can we flourish
in such a sterile room?

Honey, take us home,
so our love for her
can bloom.

The Fog

They will say
it's love at first sight.

I will tell you—
sometimes love is buried,
hidden beneath the shock of birth.

But I promise,
the fog eventually lifts.

And there it will be—
the love you both deserve.

Transition

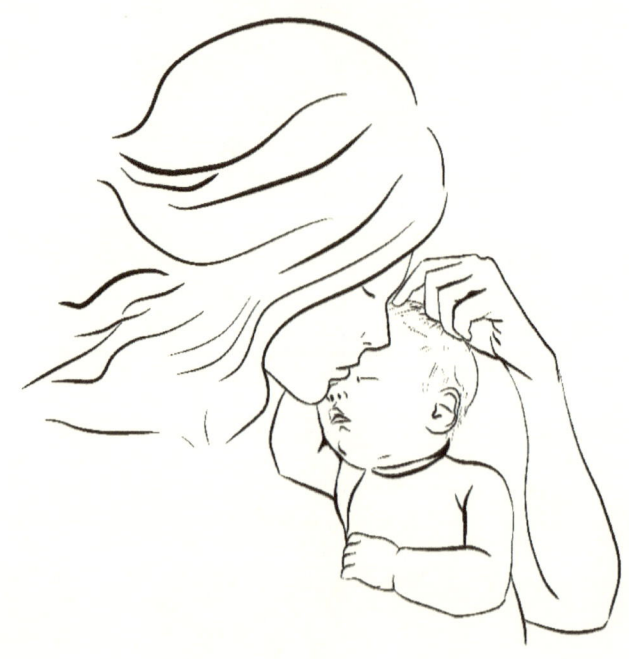

Coming Home

I settle on our couch
with you in my arms,
unable to take my eyes away.

Are you breathing?
Are you cold?
And so it begins—

The endless worries,
the constant awareness—
I am obsessed.

I cannot describe it,
the duty I feel
to connect and protect.

I close my eyes
and breathe you in—

ancient understanding
rippling through me.

Insecure

These young women pass by

tight,
toned,
and smooth.

I look down at my belly,
the empty cave
of a womb.

I'm still healing,
still deflating,

still in pain,
still integrating.

But I refuse
to feel insecure—

I created life.
I created her.

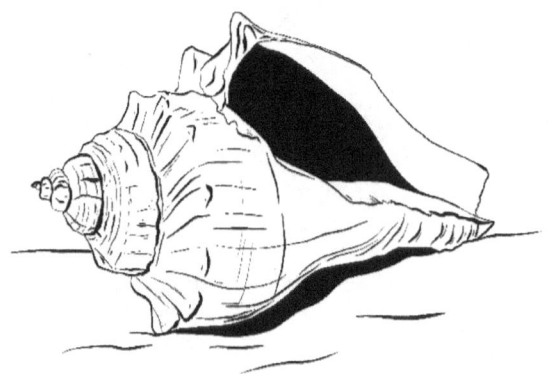

Postpartum

I gained a daughter and lost my Self.
Woman no longer,
Mother I am.

Anger rising,
confidence dwindling,
anxiety at its peak.

An empty shell
lost in the fog,
unaware of the help I need.

What About Me?

The baby is fed,
the bottles are clean,
but what about me?

The laundry is done,
the dog is walked,
but what about me?

She's crying again,
not wanting her dad,
but what about me?

I try to think
of the last time
I prioritized me.

My mind blanks
as the baby cries.

Now is not the time
to think about me.

Default Parent

You always ask me what to do—
as if I know it all.

A million questions hurled my way,
my back against the wall.

Why is it my job
to be the director of this house?

Why does it feel like
I'm parenting my own spouse?

I know you mean well,
you just want to help.

Default Parent (Continued)

But if I make one more decision,
I'll lose myself.

I'll break free—

run from this house
and into the trees—

sun in my eyes,
dirt on my feet,

answering to no one,
no one but me.

Night feeds

Another sleepless night
with you nursing on my chest.

I know I should feel grateful,
but all I crave is rest.

We rock in quiet circles
while your dad dreams undisturbed.

You feed, and I unravel
my sanity gently stirred.

Cry It Out

"Let her cry," they say.
"She needs to learn herself," they say.

But like a bear, I roar—
Protective,
hackles raised.

No—

She will learn that
when she's scared,
I will hold her.

When she's hungry,
I will feed her.

When she's lost,
I will guide her.

Cry It Out (Continued)

Motherhood
does not end
when the lights go out.

My love
does not set
with the sun.

So, I go to her,
like a moth to flame.

I will always answer—
that, she will always know.

Touched Out

My body no longer feels like mine.
She never gets a break.

Holding
Clinging
Feeding

My temper begins to shake.

She's hungry.
He's horny.
Another round of me.

I'm repulsed by your touch,
can you just let me be?

Touched Out (Continued)

The guilt crashes through me—
how dare I prioritize myself?

Putting everyone's needs
ahead of my own health.

This endless tug,
this give and take—

How much longer
before I break?

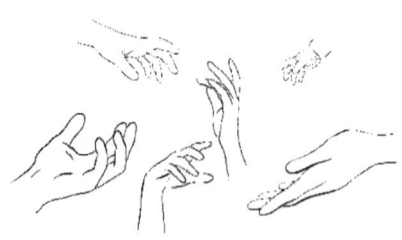

Rage

It's always there
beneath the surface,
waiting to lash out.

I'm scared of her,
she's in control,
of that, I have no doubt.

She feeds on silence,
grows with stress,
striking when I burn out.

Permission

Why do I ask for permission
to step away?

Showering
Errands
Exercise

My default is to stay.

Meanwhile, he comes and goes,
no guilt creeping in.

I begin to envy his freedom,
my patience wearing thin.

No one to blame but myself,
shackles I forged from guilt.

I'm done asking for permission,
shattering the jail I built.

Control

I tried to build you the perfect day,
and I lost my sanity along the way.

Sleep schedules,
wake windows,
feeding times too.

Thinking if I could perfect it all,
then I could perfect you, too.

But that's not how this works,
I eventually learned.

I thought I had it all figured out,
until I crashed and burned.

Whiplash

The whiplash is exhausting—
the high-contrast feelings of this.

Utterly obsessed
with the soul in front of me,

while simultaneously
daydreaming about Before.

Back when I had endless time,
endless choices,
on how to spend my days.

A quiet sigh escapes my lips.

Whiplash (Continued)

But then—
you wrap your little hand
around my finger.

The daydream slips away.
My heart swells.
My eyes dampen.

Utterly obsessed
with the soul
right in front of me.

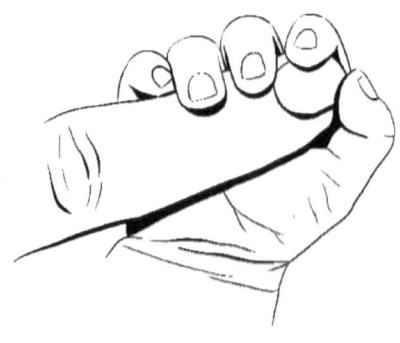

Back to Life

Silently begging
to go back to the real world.

A necessity
to separate woman from mother.

Because this past year
I have been just a mother,

a caregiver,
a feeder,
a servant,

chained to the tiny demands
dragging me through
day and night.

Back to Life (Continued)

I need to remember what it feels like
to be a woman—

a friend,
a lover,
a free body.

I ache for her—
the woman I once was.

She's buried beneath
the weight of it all,

impatiently waiting
for me to free her again.

Back to Work

Sitting at my desk,
wondering how I'm supposed to care.

I look at a picture of you,
and it doesn't seem fair.

This job feels frivolous,
these people irrelevant.

I somehow begged for this,
yet my true calling is evident.

A corporation's worst nightmare:
a workaholic turned mother.

Broke free from one leash,
only to clip on another.

Still, I keep working—
so we're not scraping by,

because everything I do,
you are my why.

Therefore So Am I

But then I clock out
and I pick her up.
She smiles,
and so do I.
Tears form in my eyes.
We play.
She's so happy—
therefore so am I.

Complete

I bring you closer,
you curl up next to me.

I can't describe this feeling,
it's something you can't see.

Like the final puzzle piece
clicking softly into place,

like coming home,
after life in a suitcase.

I feel whole,
it feels right.

I feel grounded,
no stress in sight.

I breathe you in—
my soul knows best:

you're back at home,
now she can rest.

Fatherhood

I see you working
long days each week.

I see you home at night
for hide and seek.

I see you try to balance
your needs with hers.

I see the hard memories
that fatherhood stirs.

I see you trying
to break generational cycles.

I see you breathe before speaking
when her tantrums spiral.

Fatherhood (Continued)

You're the present dad
she'll always look up to,

I don't say it enough—
how proud I am of you.

Fate was surely at play,
the night we said "I do."

Lifeline

You pulled me to shore
when I was lost at sea.

You kept me anchored
when I needed to be.

You noticed the moments
I wasn't myself,

always asking
how you can help.

Postpartum tried,
tried to drown me,

but you were there,
there to save me.

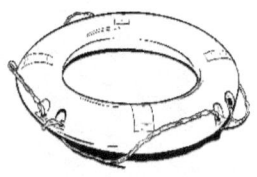

Choosing Him

I slowly take another sip of coffee,
as you and your dad giggle in bed.

I silently thank my seventeen-year-old self
for choosing him instead.

I chose a boy who made me laugh,
a boy who made me feel seen.

Now I see a man prioritizing fatherhood
and taking care of me.

Glimmers

A glimmer in the dark,
at last, I see the light.

Postpartum left its mark,
but alas, the end's in sight.

Reckoning

A Surprising Revelation

And then—
your personality
began to bloom.

You cracked a smile,
giggles escaped,
words took shape.

And with it came a sudden truth—
a surprising revelation,
unearthed at last:

the baby phase
is not for me.

A Surprising Revelation (Continued)

Now, parenting no longer
feels like guessing.

You tell me your wants,
your needs.

I get to know you,
you get to know me.

Oh, how refreshing—
how fun
this will be.

Milestone Tasks

Sitting cross-legged
on your bedroom floor,

removing the diapers
you don't need anymore.

I pause for a moment
to fully absorb—

these kinds of tasks
are easy to ignore.

To you,
I'm just clearing a drawer

To me,
I'm letting go of her before.

This version of you
is slipping away,

so I sit here a while longer,
no rush in my day.

Rush

And so we rush our days,
meeting one milestone
only to prepare for the next.

Always a step ahead,
forgetting to pause,
forgetting to breathe—

forgetting to celebrate
what's right in front of me.

Rest

You sleep on my chest,
your lips forming a smile.

Our hearts almost touching,
I could stay here a while.

There's plenty I need to do;
I could lay you in your bed.

But I'll stay here and rest,
connecting with you instead.

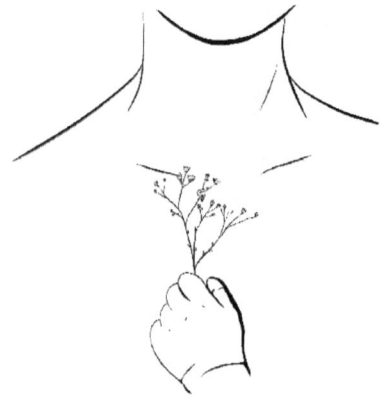

You Woke Me Up

You woke me up
from a driftless journey;
simulated and disoriented.

You woke me up;
heart reactivated,
soul illuminated,

My walking heart,
my darling daughter,
you woke me up.

Spark

You came along
and ignited a spark.

Now there are things
I'm ready to start.

New dreams bloom,
new goals take flight—

you came along,
and doubt lost its fight.

Anything I want,
I try to pursue,

hoping you learn
you can do it too.

You gave me purpose,
you gave me drive.

Because of you,
I feel alive.

The Forgotten Tribe

Before becoming a mother,
I heard ones before me complain.

Complain about their children,
the responsibility,
the lack of freedom,
the stress.

"Why have kids?"
I thought.

Oh, how naïve of me.

These women have not been complaining,
they have been silently screaming for help.

The Forgotten Tribe (Continued)

Screaming for a tribe
that has not existed in decades.

Screaming for support
from the few who truly understand.

No,
we are not meant to do this alone.

No,
you are not complaining.

You have been calling for your tribe,
and I have finally answered.

Lineage

I close my eyes
and see the women before.

The ones who carried me
before I carried you.

Mother
Grandmother
and the Greats before her.

All it took was a whisper,
and my soul began to stir.

"We had to survive.
You get to *thrive*."

Lineage (Continued)

Understanding crashed through me
as I allowed myself
a moment to weep.

For the mothers who came before—

the ones who never knew
the luxury of simply living.

I wipe my tears,
as determination floods my veins.

It is my honor—
my duty—
to mother in ways my lineage
could only dream of.

What's Passed Down

Roots of our lineage,
tangled and imperfect—
we inherit patterns
we never chose.

May we find the strength
and the awareness
to rewrite our story—

to offer ourselves
and our children
what was missing before

and what we always deserved.

Raising the Bar

Generation by generation
slowly raising the bar.

Each mother before us
did what she could,

with a simple hope
of giving her child

a lighter path to tread.

What I Didn't Receive

I pull you into a hug
as I wait for your tears to dry.

This gesture feels so profound
and I suddenly realize why.

Healing my inner child
in real time—

Comfort
Affection
Connection

Traits in your childhood
that are blurry in mine.

So I pull you in closer,
as my throat clogs with emotion.

With this quiet gesture,
I rewrite the old notion—

a mother's love,
reborn in devotion.

Just a Mother

Just a mother, I reply,
when asked what I do.

As if that is not something to take seriously.
As if I am not shaping the future.
As if that is not enough in itself.

Just a mother, I reply.

As if I did not create a body and a soul, like God himself.
As if the weight of it does not bring me to my knees.
As if the love unearthed did not feel like a spiritual awakening.

Just a mother, I reply,
a smirk spreading across my face,
pride and honor radiating from my bones.

Anew

Every day,
I found a little more of myself again.

Like puzzles pieces
scattered around the house,

I began putting back together
the woman I once was—

or so I thought.

I came to realize that
with motherhood,

you never go back,
you simply

become anew.

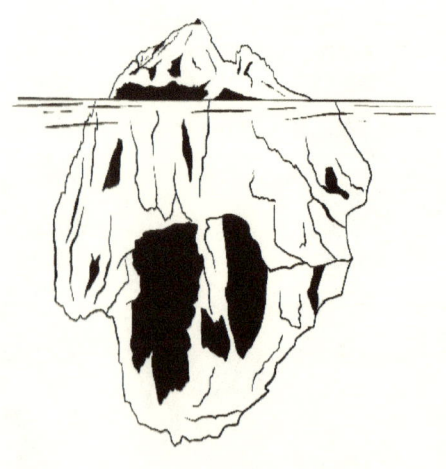

More

I thought I would go back
to who I was before.

I became who I was,
and then, became more.

My capacity for joy
grew infinitely.

The depths of my sorrow
ran deep as the sea.

Now everything I feel
cuts me to my core.

Yes, I became who I was,
and thankfully, even more.

Elevate

You can let motherhood break you,
like rust eating through a once-shiny car.

Or you can let motherhood elevate you,
like the powerful goddess that you are.

Reemergence

Rediscover

I met you
and rediscovered myself.

Putting societal pressures
back on the shelf.

You have rekindled my wonder,
my silliness,
my play.

And now—
I can't imagine
living any other way.

Bloom

Before Motherhood,
I was just a seed in the ground,
thinking this was it.

Not realizing
life hadn't even begun.

Then you arrived,
shaking me up like a storm.

I burst at the seams,
believing I was dying.

But really I was just
beginning to bloom.

Alive

You brought color to my life,
and warmth all around.

Like a plant reaching for the sun,
after a lifetime underground.

Tears

Your sorrow—
does it ache more for you,
or for me?
I do not know.

But I am certain,
that when your tears fall
my chest cracks.

We Embrace

You need a hug
and I do too.

We collide,
we embrace.

I stay as long
as it takes.

I'm never first
to let go.

I hold you tight,
just so you know—

my love for you
won't outgrow.

Your POV

We continue down the trail,
I spot the playground up ahead.

You stop once again
and focus on the ground instead.

Who am I to decide
how you should have fun?

Play was never meant to be
a to-do list to get done.

So, I release the rush,
the urge for destination.

I sit down next to you
and join your imagination.

The Ride Home

My laugh catches the breeze
and slips out the sunroof,

as my daughter and I
belt out Smash Mouth
at the top of our lungs.

Dirt beneath our nails,
sunset in our eyes,
we ride home.

Pleasantly exhausted
after a day of play.

In the rearview mirror
her smile meets mine,

and I suddenly realize
this is exactly where
I'm supposed to be.

In Sync

Moonlight creeping in,
my mind still racing from the day.

Then suddenly,
I hear your little footsteps
coming this way.

You crawl into bed,
I pull down the cover,
and you nestle in
alongside your mother.

Calm washes over,
our breath begins to sync.
And just like that,
my brain no longer needs to think.

A faint smile appears
as I drift off to sleep.
This connection with her
I hope to forever keep.

Sleeping In

I snooze my alarm
one more time,

and look over at the family
I get to call mine.

Birds begin to sing,
morning light peeking through.

I know I should wake up,
and I know you should too.

But you sleep so peacefully,
between me and your dad,

And our dog lightly snores
at the foot of the bed.

Sleeping In (Continued)

There is something so sacred
about this part of the day.

And this view is too good
to let slip away.

So I pull up the covers
and soak this in.

Why would I leave
this heaven I'm in?

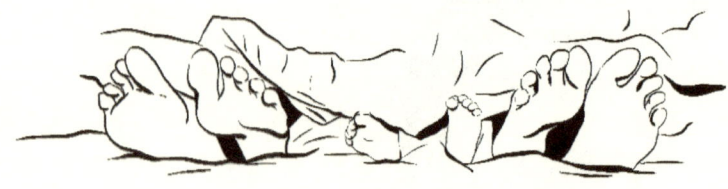

A Tuesday Afternoon

"I love you, Mommy,"
you say, mid-bite.

I look up from my plate
into your deep blue eyes.

You said it so casually,
so matter-of-fact.

My chest suddenly swells,
threatening to crack.

And just like that—
my worries dissipate,
my stresses too.

Nothing else matters
but us in this room.

I take your hand
I say "I love you too,"

as we continue eating
on a Tuesday afternoon.

Noise

Daycare,
stay at home,
nanny—
what should we do?

Homeschool,
private school,
public—
just tell me what to do.

Actually, that's the problem:
too many voices
are crowding this room.

So I block out the noise,
and close my eyes—

just long enough
to let my intuition sing.

A quiet, grounded melody
that finally tells me
exactly what to do.

Decisions

Leaving the park
after a day in the creek,
dirt and sand still cling our feet.

We drive past a field
of kids playing ball
and that's when I start to question it all.

Our parenting.
Our choices.
The way we spend our days.

Sometimes,
with parenting,
it feels like a maze.

Decisions (Continued)

Should she join a team
instead of splashing in a creek?

Should we be more structured
with how we plan our week?

But then I see
her exhausted smile,

and I think I'm okay
with our parenting style.

My Wildflower

Sometimes I wonder

if I'm raising a Tarzan
in a world of CEOs.

A lone wildflower
amid manicured lawns.

A wisp of wonder
in a world that craves order.

Still, we walk the path,
less polished, less planned.

The unbeaten trail
where wild things grow.

My Favorite Place

Let me show you
my favorite place to be.

When I was a kid,
and current-day me.

Off to woods,
we can roam free.

I look at you,
and I see little me.

Bittersweet

As you sleep on my chest,
I look back on the years.

Knowing you're getting older,
my eyes fill with tears.

You're my one and only,
every first milestone is also the last.

Yes, the days can feel slow,
but the years move too fast.

The newborn days are gone,
the last time I'll have a four-year-old.

I may have more freedom,
but only one hand to hold.

You're my one and only,
so I'll treasure each day.

As sad as it may feel,
I wouldn't have it any other way.

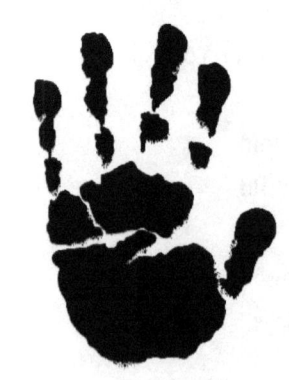

Traces

Smeared fingerprints
on the mirror
from when she was two.

I refuse to wipe them off—
enough memories
have faded from my view.

Friends

I stare at a photo of myself
at five years old.

Across the room, you play,
the same age now.

Would we have been friends?
I like to think so.

I get choked up at the thought,
of little you and little me.

I think you would have been
exactly who I needed a friend to be.

A unique soul,
unafraid of unbeaten paths.

I look up,
and watch you play,

thanking God
you're my best friend today.

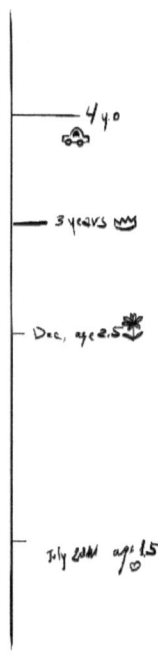

Notches on the Door Trim

"Look how tall I am!" she says,
as we view the pencil mark
just etched onto her door trim.

I stare at it, unable to register
the reality of passing time.

I take her in as she runs off
to tell her dad the exciting news.

Thin muscle travels along her limbs
where pillowed creases used to lie.

I glance out the window to the trees,
surprised to see clouds of green,
as we meet the middle of spring.

When did that happen?

Notches on the Door Trim (Continued)

Growth is happening all around me,
and I fail to notice, distracted by
the mindless rhythm of routine.

So I take in the texture of each dancing leaf,
I absorb the sound of my family,
giggling together in the kitchen.

My mind finally anchored in the now,
refusing to let this season of life
slip past me in a blur.

Five

And suddenly we're here and you're five
and I can't decide how to feel.

I'm proud of the girl you're becoming
but angry at how time can steal.

We're shopping for school supplies,
conversations becoming deep.

A toddler no longer stands before me
and all I can do is weep.

And yet—

I'm excited for this,
a new level of parenthood unlocked.

The carousel of conflicting emotions
cannot be stopped.

First Day

I take you to school
on your very first day.

I give you one last hug
and you're on your way.

You turn around
and see that I've stayed.

Tears rolling down,
I refuse to wipe away.

You look so nervous
as you begin to wave.

I smile to remind us
to both be brave.

First Day (Continued)

Then—

You run back towards me
and I drop to my knee.

I say I love you
and you love me.

My heart shatters
as I finally see—

my baby is five,
and letting go of me.

Side By Side

You're growing up
and I am too.

I'm so grateful
to do this with you.

I grab your hand;
your tether, your guide,

as we wander through life,
exploring side by side.

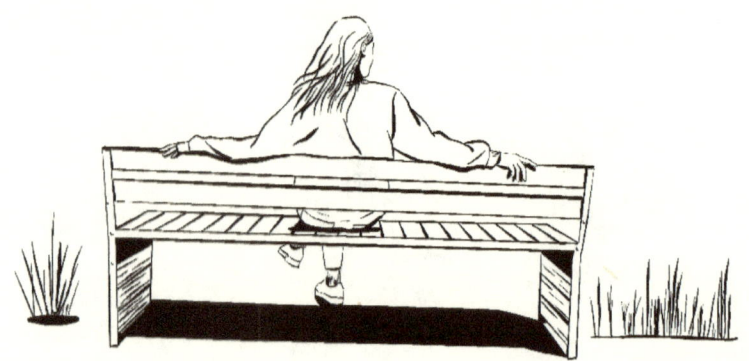

Mediocre

They will tell you to conquer the world.
Dream big, live fast,
become legendary.

Oh, but how my soul craves the mundane.
The unproductive joy of being slow.
The unprofitable peace of being in the moment.

The privilege of having nothing on my mind
but the scene unfolding in front of me,
as I watch you sprint across the playground.

A slow, steady inhale,
as I take in the aroma of freshly cut grass,
watching your dad pull you into a hug.
The love between us, a force to be reckoned with.

Mother Earth suddenly showcasing her approval,
as the sun peeks out,
rays of light and warmth spreading on our skin.

Yes, I think I will enjoy this mediocre life.
Yes, I think I will stay right here.

Integration

I kiss her goodbye
while she's playing in her room.

Grabbing my gym shoes,
I tell him I'll be back in an hour.

I catch myself in the mirror,
proud of the woman looking back.

Stronger,
wiser,
more confident,
yet more humbled.

Woman
Mother
Wife

Integration (Continued)

The integration is nearly complete.

My lips tug upward
into a savage smile.

Yes, I found the woman I was
before motherhood—
and thankfully
even more.

Author's Note

Writing this book has been a deeply transformative and healing journey for me. I started writing these when my daughter was around one, as I needed to process the extreme duality that motherhood is.

My greatest wish is that within these pages you find echoes of your own experiences or insights into the profound complexity of becoming a mother. May these words remind you that no part of this journey is traveled alone.

Thank you for allowing my story to intersect with yours. I'd love to stay connected—you can reach me at morgandaviswritings@gmail.com or find me on Instagram @morganleighdavis, where I'll share announcements about future books and projects.

Warmly,

Morgan

www.ingramcontent.com/pod-product-compliance
Lightning Source LLC
Chambersburg PA
CBHW031522120626
46545CB00005B/1951